The

Ultimate

Brexit Diary

23.06.2016-29.03.2017

S.L.C

ISBN-13: **978-1544974873**
ISBN-10: **1544974876**

Disclaimer

Beware for every truth we write or say, we hurt someone's feelings by gratifying another.

–Anonymous (7/12/2016)

(Be careful for what you wish for as you may just get it.

And with every wish granted, comes the calm before the storm.)

(Anonymous 06/07/2016)

Edward Snowden

95.9% of Gibraltar voted for EU membership. 62% of Scotland. 56% of Northern Ireland. Is this the end of the UK?

Foreword

I remember more than 6 years ago when I was attending an evening party in East London, I had a dialogue with a very interesting young man. I told him I was a writer, but sometimes I was sensitive about writing the truth and exploring true feelings, because the public reaction could be extremely negative.

His response to me was that, I am not a real writer and I am not true to myself. His words are still in my head today. And when years later I asked about his welfare, I was told he had gone to the North Pole to explore it. I think I had so much respect for him almost immediately, as I realized he followed his passion and his heart, and his dreams, without a worry in life about the opinion of others.

This is my Brexit diary and the journey of events that led to the British Exit from the EU. The diary covers the events that happened immediately after the EU referendum vote. I will share facts and true feelings of mine and the opinions of other people in this journal.

I feel extremely frustrated and disappointed that as a German citizen that has lived in Britain since the early 90s, paid my taxes and hoped one day to enjoy my state pension and retire joyfully in Britain, that I am now uncertain of my future in Britain

I and a few million European citizens are uncertain about reaping the rewards of our hard earned labour. What baffles me the most is how at least 17 million British people voted to leave the EU, without having a proper understanding of the consequence of their actions!

Didn't these people care about their friends, their children or the families they would break up over-night? Didn't these people think about their future? And all this talk about taking back control which became the leave campaign slogan really must have won the hearts of these 17million people.

But what we are really experiencing today is multiculturalism which is here to stay no matter what decisions we make as individuals or as a Country. Multiculturalism is here to stay and grow globally.

In my opinion, the dreams of our younger generation have been ignored and destroyed by a friendship rivalry, which should have remained as a friendship rivalry between Boris and David. This friendship rivalry should never have been allowed to spill out to the British political scene, where other opportunists took advantage to manipulate this situation into a new chess Brexit game.

I can only imagine that there are more than 3 million EU citizens in this Country who are extremely gutted and disappointed. Please read my journal and understand our pain.

What is the European Union?

The European Union has 28 member states and it was established on the 1st of November 1993 in Maastricht, Netherlands. Its current headquarters is in Brussels, Belgium. It currently has an estimated population of at least 508 million people.

The European Union was mainly founded for a low a single market that encouraged the free flow of movement of people, goods, services and capital within it. Inside the EU, passport controls have been eradicated and a single monetary system has also been established since 1999. It means all member States enjoy and share a single currency known as the Euro.

The EU formed as a result of the European Economic Community (EEC). The EEC was formed in 1958 and initially had only 6 countries as members: Belgium, France, Italy, Luxembourg, the Netherlands and West Germany. The UK joined the EEC in 1973 and held a referendum in 1975. The result of that referendum was 67% of the British voters wanted to stay in the EEC.

Current members of the European Union are as follows;

Austria	Belgium	Bulgaria
EU member: 1 January 1995	**EU member:** 1 January 1958	**EU member:** 1 January 2007
Capital: Vienna	**Capital:** Brussels	**Capital:** Sofia
Currency: Euro.	**Currency:** Euro.	**Currency:** Bulgari an lev BGN
Croatia	Cyprus	Czech Republic
EU member: 1 July 2013	**EU member:** 1 May 2004	**EU member:** 1 May 2004
Capital: Zagreb	**Capital:** Nicosia	**Capital:** Prague
Currency: Croatia n Kuna HRK	**Currency:** Euro.	**Currency:** Czech koruna (CZK)
Denmark	Estonia	Finland
EU member: 1		**EU member:** 1

January 1973 **Capital:** Copenhagen **Currency:** Danish krone DKK	**EU member:** 1 May 2004 **Capital:** Tallinn **Currency:** Euro.	January 1995 **Capital:** Helsinki **Currency:** Euro.
France **EU member:** 1 January 1958 **Capital:** Paris **Currency:** Euro.	Germany **EU member:** 1 January 1958 **Capital:** Berlin **Currency:** Euro.	Greece **EU member:** 1 January 1981 **Capital:** Athens **Currency:** Euro.
Hungary **EU member:** 1 May 2004 **Capital:** Budapest	Ireland **EU member:** 1 January 1973 **Capital:** Dublin	Italy **EU member:** 1 January 1958 **Capital:** Rome

Currency: Hungarian Forint HUF	Currency: Euro.	Currency: Euro.
Latvia **EU member:** 1 May 2004 **Capital:** Riga **Currency:** Euro.	Lithuania **EU member:** 1 May 2004 **Capital:** Vilnius **Currency:** Euro.	Luxembourg **EU member:** 1 January 1958 **Capital:** Luxembourg **Currency:** Euro.
Malta **EU member:** 1 May 2004 **Capital:** Valletta **Currency:** Euro.	The Netherlands **EU member:** 1 January 1958 **Capital:** Amsterdam **Currency:** Euro.	Poland **EU member:** 1 May 2004 **Capital:** Warsaw **Currency:** Polish Złoty PLN

Portugal	Romania	Slovakia
EU member: 1 January 1986	**EU member:** 1 January 2007	**EU member:** 1 May 2004
Capital: Lisbon	**Capital:** Bucharest	**Capital:** Bratislava
Currency: Euro.	**Currency:** Roman ian Leu RON	**Currency:** Euro.
Slovenia	Spain	Sweden
EU member: 1 May 2004	**EU member:** 1 January 1986	**EU member:** 1 January 1995
Capital: Ljubljana	**Capital:** Madrid	**Capital:** Stockhol m
Currency: Euro.	**Currency:** Euro.	**Currency:** Swedis h krona SEK

United Kingdom **EU member:** 1 January 1973 **Capital:** London **Currency:** pound sterling GBP		

The British "Brexit" referendum EU story.

The British Brexit story is one you must read from many perspectives including mine.

One of the main Brexit players was David Cameron and the other was Boris Johnson. In my opinion, the latter, Boris Johnson needed tools and people to win his little game of 'Thrones' with David. He struck his blow early in the year of 2016, much to David Cameron's surprise.

And I am not the only one that felt this was the case.

http://www.newstatesman.com/politics/elections/2016/02/why-far-referendum-concerned-it-really-all-about-boris-and-dave

The title of this article is 'Why as far as the referendum is concerned, it really all is about Boris and (Dave)'

And another article I found interesting was;

http://www.nytimes.com/2016/07/01/world/europe/boris-johnson-brexit-conservatives.html?_r=0

So look at the words highlighted in quotes from the website above and you can smell the constant rivalry between these two men.

> *'Mr. Cameron has always been threatened by Mr. Johnson; his efforts to slough off the mayor as a kind of amusing Tory mascot never worked. But it wasn't until Mr. Johnson betrayed the prime minister by throwing his support behind the Brexit campaign that the party saw the extent of his ambition.'*

The ambition to be a Prime Minister was in my opinion Boris ambition. He probably envied his friend for holding such a respectable powerful political position and he wanted to be in the Prime Minister's shoes at all cost, even if it meant back-stabbing David Cameron behind his back.

Boris Johnson is known to have charisma and a way with words and could easily sway a British population, especially with his experience of being a journalist. The newspapers and media were his greatest tools during the 'Leave' campaign, as he used it effectively to persuade a 17 million British voters.

And with all rivalry, are always opportunists. From my perspective, Nigel Farage saw the rivalry as a career opportunity and decided to join the little game at a later stage. Nigel then used questionable methods to promote some aspects of the 'leave' campaign.

To begin to understand the rivalry, I wish I could dedicate a chapter to the great 'Boris and Dave' story, because it is important to understand this to see why this referendum result should not even be considered in the first place. It is like going to a shop to buy a much needed car, but in the end being persuaded by the sales man to buy a plane instead, that you know you will never need as there are no places to park a plane in your work place.

Unfortunately this is my journal and I don't want to waste my time on a friendship rivalry between 2 men that commenced more than 30 years ago. David and Boris were part of a club called Bullingdon which was an unofficial rich male club based in Oxford. The club has a lot of history with drinking, parties, hooliganism and mischief.

In 1987, there was a picture on the internet which showed some of its members, and in that picture you could see Boris and David posing in it amongst other members. You can see that their friendship and association goes way back into the 80s. Over the years they have competed and tried to outshine each other and finally the Brexit campaign may have broken this friendship.

I think David has always been envious that he does not have the public personality and charisma that Boris has. On the other hand I feel strongly that Boris has always been envious that David has held the most prestigious political job in England. And this personal conflict spilled out during the campaign. There are so many internet articles that explain this but I just picked one at random.

http://www.theguardian.com/politics/2016/may/02/david-cameron-says-friendship-with-boris-johnson-damaged-by-brexit

'David Cameron says friendship with Boris Johnson damaged by Brexit

> The PM tells Glamour magazine that the student
> friends are 'not as close' after the London
> mayor's decision to join the Leave campaign'

But let's explain how the referendum began.

David Cameron announced the 23rd of June as a referendum date, for deciding if the British public wanted to leave or remain in the EU. He made this announcement on the 20th of February 2016. It was at this moment that MPs decided to back either the 'Leave' or the 'Remain' campaign.

And it was soon after this moment that David Cameron probably felt the pain of being back-stabbed as he watched Boris Johnson and Michael Gove back the 'Leave' campaign. Earlier on in the year it is rumoured he had been reassured by Boris that he would be supported.

Please read this carefully and ponder. The EU referendum is non-legally binding. But when the results of the votes came in, every politician was adamant that Britain is leaving and a second referendum would not be considered. I have not yet heard anyone touch this subject in detail, not even Theresa May.

On the 23rd of June the referendum took place and at 10.00pm the counting began. By the next day at 6.00am, the results were announced. 51.9 % (17,410,742) of the votes were to leave the EU, while 48.1 % (16,141,241) of votes were to stay in the EU.

The entire country was in Brexit turmoil, but what was even more surprising was that the result was a huge surprise to Boris Johnson and some of his campaigners.

In my opinion it was just a game to them, especially for Boris, and therefore they never reckoned with a win, and it is even clear they had no plan for this dream that they had sold to their 17 million supporters.

In a few days panic set in, Boris withdrew from the Conservative leadership party race, millions of pounds were wiped off the financial markets in England and the fate of over 3 million EU citizens and also millions of British citizens and families abroad became uncertain. In one single day, the plight of masses of families around the EU would be broken because of a few people like Boris Johnson, Nigel Farage and Michael Gove.

To start the process of leaving the EU, Article 50 has to be invoked but David Cameron decided to play one more rivalry joker card. He resigned and left that responsibility to his successor. It was almost as if he was saying, *'Boris you caused this mess. You wanted my job. Now you have got my job, so you trigger this Article 50 button, because I will not answer to the people of Britain in 5 years, when dreams have perished and all that is left is a stream of millions of broken and unhappy EU and British families and individuals'*.

David Cameron resigned on the 24th of June, and in a few days in my opinion, Boris plays a new game with the help of his friend Michael Gove, who comes out publicly to backstab him. But think about this. This was all a big circus show in my opinion. This was the only way a person could bow out with dignity, still have their career intact for future prospects.

Don't forget that Boris Johnson is a great storyteller and writer. The same way the public bought into his wonderful promises of leaving the EU, by Nigel and Boris promising a hilarious story of £350 million of NHS money, is the same way a new story of 'Gove backstabbing' was cooked up in few hours.

In my mind Boris did not have the courage to trigger that Article 50 and Michael Gove had to help his friend, as he knew Boris would probably win the conservative leadership easily.

I don't think Theresa May stood a chance against Boris. The only way Michael Gove could save his friend was to publicly backstab him to give Boris a possibility in future of becoming the next Prime Minister of Britain or perhaps the next leader of the Conservative party. And perhaps when the new PM, Theresa May has done all the hard work, then in the future Boris could just step in and get handed the easiest task of all.

In my opinion, there are also possibilities that Nigel and Boris may have received death threats which could have also resulted in this elaborate backstabbing plan, so as to gain some sympathy amongst the public especially by those thousands of people who were hurt.

In my opinion it is a smart move from Boris. He is worried about his personal safety but also wants to safeguard his future political prospects. He is also conscious of the fact that he cannot deliver his great promises to the British public who voted to leave the EU. Imagine if he was Prime Minister, every day he would wake up from bed worried and stressed. He will be secretly asking himself if it was all worth it. This was his last minute personal Brexit plan.

Now even in wars or conflict, there are big winners and losers. Suddenly a whole new group of individuals that were not part of this rivalry in the first place are now spilling out into the British political field as big winners or big losers.

As for the labour party leader, Jeremy Corbyn, I personally think he will destroy the reputation of the 'Labour' party. He did not put up any convincible fight for the 'Remain' campaign which makes me wonder where his real interests lay in the first place. Was it with the 'Leave' campaign?

On a last note, many times politicians are only interested about their personal ambitions and making statistics look great.

This Conservative party came into power, reduced budgets, created massive job cuts and increased University fees tremendously and yet there was no referendum. Affected people and families have suffered in silence, and it is these same affected people that voted to leave the EU, without really understanding where the economic damage originated from in the first place.

There is a saying that you must try to understand history or the danger is if you don't then history will only repeat itself.

So this is a brief personal analysis and you can choose to disagree with it. But here starts my Brexit diary which covers the Brexit journey right from the vote to the day Article 50 is officially triggered.

June 2016

Thursday, 23rd of June 2016

I knew the EU referendum voting was going to happen today and I probably intuitively knew the result already. It was 7.00am and I was getting ready for work and I was completely stressed and anxious. You didn't have to be a genius to work it all out. In the last few days of the 'Leave campaign' the 'Leave' campaigners had put adverts in the front and back page of the Metro paper with strong words of why Britain should leave the EU. Almost every major newspaper I touched in my local shop seemed to have adverts supporting the 'Leave' campaign'.

For the last few weeks, left, right and centre, in train stations, on the internet, in markets, were people actively handing out leaflets campaigning strongly for people to support the 'Leave' campaigners. I really thought there was not enough effort or a proper competitive strategy from the 'Remain' campaign group.

There were TV adverts showing just British people waiting for NHS services being compared to

Multicultural people waiting for NHS services. There was a picture of thousands of immigrants plastered on the Metro's newspaper a few days ago with some punch line statement that could persuade any person or family who was having a hard time financially.

Just imagine, a large number of the UK population read this paper every morning. It's a free newspaper and that for me was the killer joker card. It also made me feel that this was a racist campaign, and that the people behind these stories and pictures and adverts should be held accountable in court for using racism to promote their campaign.

I just couldn't understand why the 'Remain' campaigners could not counter-attack these adverts immediately the next day. I knew the last minute adverts and the FrontPage news on a few national newspapers in the last few days would be the decisive winner for the 'Leave' campaign.

I was worried, I was scared and I was stressed. I was so stressed that I was up all night and did not sleep until 4.00am when it was obvious that my predictive result would come true.

Friday, 24th of June 2016

I was up until 4.00am and at this time I decided to go to bed because it was clear that the 'Leave' campaign was leading by more than half a million votes. I kept checking the results on the internet.

There was no miracle that would allow the 'Remain' campaign to win. I sighed as I slept for just 2 hours around 4.00am and slowly begun to think about my future here in the United Kingdom.

I woke up feeling a little different with great frustration and disappointment. I felt sorry for myself and then after careful reflection, I thought about so many millions of EU citizens and British citizens in Europe that would be feeling the same I did.

I remember going to work on the train and trying to keep calm. But I could not help looking around me to watch other people's body languages. And when I looked around, my train was jam-packed with people from all Nations of the World.

This was really confusing to me because most of these commuters were legally British. So welcome to the 'World of Multiculturalism' and this referendum result will not make a difference to giving back Britain to the people of Britain. Because the face of Britain has changed in the last 50 years but many people will only understand multiculturalism later when Britain is finally out of the EU.

The leavers or those who voted to leave will then look round themselves and wonder, but we still have towns full of multicultural people, and then perhaps they will realize that the EU was never really the problem with regards to migration. Actually the EU has been extremely useful financially to Britain which has only prospered since the 90s.

Already there are hate crimes springing up everywhere in the Country and the irony of that is that some British people are the target. Some people who voted to leave the EU are already waking up and can see that this is not going to get rid of the multicultural face of Britain. Multiculturalism has been long here in Britain before the EU moved into Britain. And with families reproducing and growing each day, the face of Britain will be even more multicultural in the future! No one can ever claim or promise to get the old Britain back! It is too late for that!

Let me share a text dialogue from someone.

Mr Alan wrote a poem using a song from the Beatles

Yesterday
The chance of Brexit seemed so far away
Now it seems Farage is here to stay
Oh I believe in yesterday!

Suddenly
We are half as great as we used to be
Boris' shadow is hanging over me
Oh I believe in yesterday!

Why we
Had to go, I don't know: they couldn't say
We've done something wrong
Now I long for yesterday!

Yesterday
All the lies and all the games they played
Now I need a place to hide away
Oh I believe, in yesterday!

Let me summarize what happened very quickly. By the time I woke up and was ready to go to work, I looked at the news and it was confirmed that at 6.00am UK had voted to leave the European Union. Leave won by 52% to

48%. By the end of the day it was claimed by many news sources that at least $2 trillion had been wiped of the global financial market.

The pound also dropped significantly in value. David Cameron resigned saying he would leave the next Prime Minister of Britain to deal with the Brexit. At the same time the leader of the Labour party, Jeremy Corbyn was pressured by his people within his party to step down, and some of his people stated he was very weak during the referendum campaign.

Just one beautiful day of British politics provided so much entertainment. I think the word weak is not appropriate at all for Jeremy Corbyn. For me the word is ineffective. I feel he was absolutely and fundamentally ineffective during the campaign. If such a man could not have a great impact on the campaign then how can he actually lead a party and win any election?

Saturday, 25th of June 2016

Today I was full of pain and later my brother and his wife came to visit me to provide words of comfort about the EU Brexit reassuring me that the rights of 3 million EU citizens will be protected. His words seemed assuring but I was still sad.

I had this poem in my head which is about a man with a thousand egos. You really have to be a deep spiritual person to understand it.

A Thousand Egos

Glimmer Slimmer Dimmer
Glitter Wither Bitter
I am swimming with my ego
Sinking deep as if there is no flow
Did you know?
I have a thousand egos

Glimmer Slimmer Dimmer
Glitter Wither Bitter
Don't talk to me low
I don't want to know
I don't want a row or a blow
You may raise your eyebrows
For I am swimming with my ego

I desire a brexit
I wish an exit
My competitors have admitted defeat
My long term personal goals are neat
The masses have no wit
So I shall laugh and sit

I have a thousand egos
That tell me compromise is a 'no no no'
I have a thousand egos, that say stubbornness is the flow
Perhaps for my ego there is no tomorrow
But the seeds I sow will hurt many quite slow
That for sure is a fact I quietly know

Glimmer Slimmer Dimmer
Glitter Wither Bitter
Soon many will cry for yesterday
And I will sigh silently for a better day

Well the first signs of racism are already being reported in the news. This I feel was encouraged by some of the 'Leave' campaigners like Nigel. Apparently yesterday on the 24th of June 2016, a polish School in Cambridgeshire had the words 'Leave the EU. No more Polish vermin' post on a sign, and there were similar signs plastered around homes and schools in Huntington. On Sunday the London office of the Polish Social and Cultural Association had racist graffiti painted on it.

And even as far as Wales, a Muslim woman was told by some strangers to leave the country even though she was legally British. There were stories everywhere of foreigners in supermarkets, buses and on the street being told by strangers and other people to leave this Country.

Let us not make any mistakes about this sudden racist development. Although a large number of the targets are the Polish Community, unless Britain remain in the EU, this racist development may extend to other minority groups including the legally born and bred British people who are from the Common Wealth Countries.

And why is that you may ask? The answer is simple. It is possible that it has been there for a long time but hidden silently in the souls and hearts of many, and their true feelings only came out as they were inspired by the likes of Nigel. If this is not the case then why did they have to use dirty campaigning tricks that played on such negative emotions of the people?

Sunday, 26th of June 2016

Today was a quiet day of reflection. The news in the papers has been quiet. It is almost as if David, Boris and Nigel have secretly gone into hiding until things calm down. There is an article in the guardian explaining how Boris Johnson will rule the conservative party if he won.

There is also an article in his weekly Telegraph column, where Boris Johnson is suggesting that Brexit will not be rushed and he is also dismissing Nicola's call for a second Scottish independence referendum. Why is Boris saying Brexit should not be rushed when just a few days ago he was fighting for this Brexit phenomenon so viciously? Why switch and switch sides each time there is a challenging situation?

Monday, 27th of June 2016

The paper today was all about the current Labour leader Jeremy Corbyn. He has had to fight for his position within his party after so many resignations and protests about his weak leadership. But Jeremy is ready to hold onto his position even if it means destroying his Labour party.

He has announced a new cabinet. Only on Sunday the 26th of June, he lost 12 members of his shadow cabinet. Today he has lost more shadow ministers. Most people have criticised his EU referendum campaign efforts. I think his involvement and input clearly suggests that his heart was probably with the 'Leave Brexit' campaign or he perhaps he is just a weak leader. For me it is one or the other.

Promises promises promises

Excuses Excuses Excuses

In the papers, the First Minister of Scotland and the leader of the Scottish National Party, Nicola Sturgeon, claims that she would fight to block Brexit. I think she will have a hard fight with little support. I personally admire her political courage and I can say she is a woman of integrity. She kind of reminds me of Angela Merkel of Germany. It is only a very strong woman that can attempt to fight a lone battle. A battle with very little support!

Tuesday, 28th of June 2016

Today I read that at 4.36pm, there was a notion of no confidence in Labour leader, Jeremy Corbyn. It was passed on by his party's MPs. There was a vote of 172-40, however this vote is not legally binding. One has to laugh. It appears everything is not legally binding except the Brexit. Mr Corbyn refuses to resign so it is time to seat back and watch a circus show. There is no relevant news about the Brexit. The general atmosphere in London shows that people are still recovering from the Brexit

Wednesday, 29th of June 2016

Today is like almost the beginning of an exciting era in the journey of the Brexit. There are many questions on people's lips. Who will be England's new Prime Minister and many will say Boris Johnson is the right man for the job.

The newspapers are all speculating and weighing each of the candidates who could be the next Prime Minister of England. In the meantime David Cameron has turned to attack as the best form for defence, as he blames the EU for the Brexit vote.

The Sun newspaper which by the way is owned by Rupert Murdoch suggests Boris Johnson is winning the race. Do you remember the famous international hacking story in 2011 involving Rebekah Brooks, the former editor of the *News of the World* and former chief executive of News International? Well this Sun has vigorously backed the 'Leave' campaign that it makes me wonder who the big players behind this campaign are. Apparently she is now the CEO of News UK, which was formerly known as News International.

According to sources, David Cameron said it is the EUs policy on mass migration that frustrated Britain. OK perhaps it frustrated Britain but let us be frank all European countries were in the same position because of the general situation in Africa and Syria. Are we not to stand together and support one another in moments of difficulty and not just good times? Why do some people think it is OK to cherry pick?

Thursday, 30th of June 2016

So here comes the first political joke and shocker of the day as a media report writes 'Boris Johnson out of Conservative leadership contest'. The cards have been switched and a new political script has been written!

The summary of it all is his friend Mr Gove who worked so hard with him during the Brexit Campaign decided to back stab him and withdraw his support for Boris, for the leadership contest. Mr Gove also put himself forward as a candidate for the leadership race taking away most of Boris supporters with him.

I don't know who told this man called Mr Gove that he had any chance of winning the leadership contest. No one has heard his name or knows him. **Do you know this man called Michael Gove?** Does this make you wonder what's going on? Surely there is a big possibility here that this was staged by Boris and Gove.

In the meantime protest marches are being organised on social media and there is a reported 30000+ people taking part in one of these protests possibly on Saturday, marching from Park Lane towards Parliament Square.

So many people are airing their views about the impact of Britain leaving the EU. The US President Barack Obama has expressed concerns about the long-term economic global growth between Britain and Countries around the World globally.

I think the main question now is who is the next Prime Minister going to be and when will Article 50 be invoked? What will it mean to the EU citizens currently living and working in Britain? What will it mean to British citizens that live in other parts of the EU?

July 2016

Friday, 1st July 2016

A Country in turmoil

I decided to give my entry in the journal a title today because I see Britain as a country in turmoil today. The Country is without a serious leader. Backstabbing is going on within the conservative party. Mr Gove is now making silly speeches, looking even more silly by the minute, that one cannot even take him seriously as a politician. Mr Corbyn is stubbornly hanging on to his labour crown like a stubborn old man who lives by the bible of principles.

The media and internet is full with stories about each one of these topics so we shall see what the next few days bring us. I sincerely hope it will be a breath of fresh Brexit air.

Saturday, 2nd July 2016

Today the media is quiet and the atmosphere is generally quiet about the Brexit. The streets of London are the same. Thousands of people have begun their protest march through the streets of London to protest against the referendum result to leave the EU. The demonstrators met at Park Lane, and it was a historic moment as more than 30,000 people begun their walk towards the Parliament Square. The idea of the protest is to stop the government from triggering Article 50.

It is strange because I never really knew about Article 50 and what it stands for until this year and I believe there are millions of people just like me that have just recently acquainted themselves with Article 50.

Sunday, 3rd July 2016

Alright I read this article today and the headlines are 'Michael Gove: 'I woke up early and decided to run for PM.'

http://www.bbc.co.uk/news/uk-politics-36697793

If you then go to the web link above you will see how he explains that Boris does not have what it takes to be Prime Minister of Britain. How ironic, if Boris does not have what it takes then what makes Mr Gove think he even has half of what Boris has to run for the Prime Minister position.

Did he smoke something strange and wake up this morning seeing a different dimension that the whole World is not seeing? Which 'La La La ' land or planet does Mr Gove think he is living in? Perhaps when the effects of whatever he has taken wears off, he will come back to the reality zone.

Monday, 4th July 2016

Today headlines where made when Nigel Farage said he was standing down as leader of the UK Independence Party (UKIP).

When I read that Nigel had resigned my first reaction was how convenient! He does not even believe in his own cause or dream. He and Boris fed their personal dreams to 17 million British people and now they are abandoning all the people that believed in this fairy tale of getting their old Britain back. They are not staying to play a major role in getting back Britain.

I cannot understand why people all over Britain that voted leave cannot take a good look around them, and see that British people are diverse.

By voting to leave the EU, Britain is still going to have multi-cultural people who are legally British that reside in this country for a life time. People need to wake up to understand that multi-culturalism is here to stay forever in Britain and the EU is so necessary to create jobs for the masses of multi-cultural British people.

I personally think it is an absolute shame that self-attention seekers and drama queens get to sell a false dream to people and run away when masses of people actually buy into that dream and depend on them to execute a dream.

Another article is one where the government has been criticised for not ensuring the rights of EU citizens to remain in the UK after the country leaves the EU.

There is another article which explains that some individuals are looking at legal steps to ensure the 'House of Commons' vote on Article 50

http://www.bbc.co.uk/news/uk-politics-36700350

Tuesday, 5th of July 2016

So racism has escalated around England since the Brexit result. The Headlines were 'Man rips off Muslim mum's veil and tells her: "Live by British rules" in front of young son'

Source:http://www.mirror.co.uk/news/uk-news/man-rips-muslim-mums-veil-8354017

Other headline are 'Andrea Leadsom: EU citizens in UK are not bargaining chips.'

http://www.bbc.co.uk/news/uk-politics-36701856

EU Commission President Jean-Claude Juncker shares my vision which I highlighted in an early entry in my diary, when he accused Brexit campaigners Boris Johnson and Nigel Farage of quitting when things got difficult. I am glad there are people out there that share the same view that these men are not leaders.

He said "The Brexit heroes of yesterday are now the sad Brexit heroes of today," he told the European Parliament.

Also the last news for the day was that Theresa May won the first round of Conservative leadership election. This is not surprising at all as she no longer has any more competition.

Wednesday, 6th of July 2016

Things have cooled down. I guess everyone is playing the waiting game. The European citizens living in the UK, are so uncertain about their future here. Every day when I read the news, I am hoping to read something positive or encouraging or even hopeful. It is so sad that a couple or shall I say a few politicians have changed the future destiny of Britain forever.

Well while all this is going on, they are slugging it out in the Conservative party. And the Labour party has a different fight where Jeremy is stubbornly refusing to step down from his position even after massive resignations in the last few days. Good luck to him, I will be voting for the Conservative party. So I am switching. I have switched sides' over-night. I am doing what I call a 'Boris switching'. And perhaps I will soon switch to SNP where we probably have one of the only most influential leaders of today still standing.

The news is that Andrea Leadsom and Michael Gove are fighting it out to join Home Secretary Theresa May on the course to become the next Conservative leader and Prime Minister of Britain.

I have this feeling Michael Gove already knows he would be a loser before he joined this contest. So there must be another reason why he is taking part in this political contest. Perhaps to make the Boris backstabbing story even more believable!

Thursday, 7th of July 2016

It is strange that since the EU referendum, I have been waking up each day to read the news in anticipation for something miraculous, yet I cannot really place my finger on what it is. I mean it is possible that Britain is not going to have a new Prime minister until October 2016. Anything we hear now is just speculation and the real Brexit juice may only start rolling from the 1st of October 2016.

Whenever I am writing about this Brexit journey, I am kind of reminded of the book 'A Woman in Berlin'. When you read that book, you will see that everything happened so quickly. But in the days that built up to the Russian occupation of Berlin, most German people were playing the waiting game and hoping that nothing terrible would happen. The clever and cautious women had already begun hiding their daughters in their basements, and some women had begun to put on a disguise to pose as men.

The Brexit kind of makes me think back to the Russian occupation of Berlin. As an EU citizen, what should you do to protect yourself and future from a terrible stroke of calamity or uncertainty in Britain?

Theresa May's recent statement is really worrying when she says she cannot guarantee the rights of EU citizens. Overnight Theresa is telling the World that she cannot guarantee the rights of EU citizens already living and working in Britain. What is even more frustrating is she is not even insisting that she will fight for the rights of the EU citizens that live and work here. Whose side is she on? I thought she supported the remain campaign!

Today's news has major headlines about Blair's story, of how he knowingly deceived the British public and made the UK go to war with Iraq knowing fully well that Saddam had no weapons of mass destruction. Think about how many people protested during that period and how the voices of the people were ignored. And the Chilcot report which has taken 9 years to write is telling us what so many people already knew way back then.

Then there is the story (Sky news) of Michael Gove, of the Conservative party, playing dirty tricks to win more votes by texting MPs that are already supporting Theresa May to switch to his side.

I all I want to know right now is what is going to happen to the EU citizens living and working in Britain.

Also the second round of voting for the Conservative leader is to take place today. So perhaps by the end of today we can have that clown of a character thrown out so that it is down to two women fighting for the leadership of the Conservative party.

I also ready a story (Business Insider UK - 3rd July) about Jeremy Corbyn receiving money from Iran which deserves an explanation. Also in another story, the Labour rebels have finally admitted that they cannot remove Jeremy Corbyn as party leader.

Again this old stubborn politician is receiving too much attention in the media. All I am asking myself is 'Doesn't the Labour party want to win the next election?'

I think for most of EU citizens, we are waiting for the drama to be over with the Conservative party. We want Theresa May elected quickly and then let us know our faith quickly. She was on the 'Remain' campaign, but in the last few days where she has grown in confidence clearly knowing that she has a clear chance to be a new prime Minister of England, she is clearly singing a song to me that favours those who voted to leave the UK.

By the end of the day, 2 contenders from the conservative party will go forward in a vote of about 150,000 Conservative members. The winner will be the new Prime Minister of Britain and it is suggested by news that results will be announced on the 9th of September.

Friday, 9th of July 2016

I woke up today feeling really good. I quickly checked the Euro 2016 football results and saw that Germany lost to France by 2 goals. Minutes later I was heading for breakfast at my local café. Once there I picked up the 'Sun' newspaper hoping to read anything that was relevant to the Brexit. Instead 5 pages of the entire 'Sun' newspaper were dedicated to the Blair story and the Chilcot report.

Page 26 has a whole page dedicated to how to have amazing sex. There is nothing at all that is relevant to the Brexit in this paper today.

This is how the media manipulates. I call it 'pure manipulation of the masses'. Masses of people are made by the media to forget about what was important just a few days.

Only a few days ago, everything in Britain was about leaving the EU and now today, there is not even one story related to the EU, the Brexit, the Conservative party or even the Labour party in the Sun newspaper.

Who owns this newspaper? And coincidentally in my opinion this newspaper supported the 'Leave' campaign with articles during the campaign

But after trawling the internet for some news, I finally found someone who is as bold as I am, and I think we are on the same wave length. The only difference is that he is famous so people will listen and read about what he has to say.

http://www.huffingtonpost.co.uk/entry/john-hannah-backs-independence-for-scotland-and-compares-britain-to-nazi-germany_uk_577e33a0e4b07a99eadc0a6e?yptr=yahoo&ref=yfp

And its 15:12pm and Home Secretary Theresa May (199 Votes) and Energy Minister Andrea Leadsom (84 Votes), are going to fight for the leadership of Britain's governing party. The winner will make history by becoming Britain's second female Prime Minister. The result should be announced on the 9th of September 2016, after 150,000 Conservative Party members decide by voting who their winner is.

Saturday, 9th of July 2016

Today is another day where the newspapers are quiet. The papers have slowed down. There is nothing to write about. 2 women are fighting it out in the Conservative party to be the next Prime Minister. Andrea Leadsom is saying because she is a mother she will make a better Prime Minister. I am sure that must really hurt Theresa

May as she has does not have children. I have no idea if that is a personal choice or if she has not been lucky. Well the good old saying that 'women can be bitches' is not really wrong.

David Cameron is being accused of being power drunk and holding onto power. Apart from that there is nothing else in the paper regarding the EU. This is the calm before the storm.

Sunday, 10th of July 2016

I woke up this morning and trawled the internet and saw this article where Mathew Parris talks about his disappointment. I will paste the article at the end just in case the link disappears.

Let us not forget the lovely Mother of two children that lost her life on the 16th of June, 2016.

https://www.theguardian.com/uk-news/2016/jun/16/labour-mp-jo-cox-shot-in-west-yorkshire

http://www.spectator.co.uk/2016/07/for-the-first-time-in-my-life-i-feel-ashamed-to-be-british/?ref=yfp

Part of the article

'For the first time in my life, I feel ashamed to be British. I've seen a nasty side to our national character, and seen colleagues and friends pander to it in a way I never thought they would.'

Matthew Parris

But these last few months I've seen a Britain, specifically an England, that I simply do not like. I've seen a nasty side, and seen colleagues and friends pander to it in a way I never thought they would. It has made me feel lonely in my own country, and the experience has touched me irreparably.

The reliance of the leaders and opinion leaders of the Leave campaign upon resentment of foreigners, dislike of immigration and — in many cases — hatred of immigrants, has been absolutely disgraceful. It should be a stain upon our conscience.

The day of the referendum result, I was waiting outside the tent where CNN were filming on College Green near Parliament. In front of the camera I saw two people shouting at each other and sensed the argument was out of control. Next up for interview, I sat down to watch. The interviewer was Christiane Amanpour, her interviewee the MEP Daniel Hannan.

I have never seen so violent an argument on TV. Nobody won but both lost their tempers. Amanpour accused Hannan of trying to win the Leave campaign by inciting hatred of immigrants; Hannan insisted he had never done so, had never even argued against immigration, but simply for Britain to 'take back control'. Shouting, he challenged Amanpour to cite any example of anti-immigrant language he had ever used.

Over the last few months a poison has been seeping through our national life. My faith in my fellow English, in our democracy, and in those who serve it in high places led me wholly to underestimate its potency or its capacity to spread.

'You just don't get it, do you?' Brexiteers have crowed to me: 'You're out of touch.' They are right. I was. I did not know my own country. I do now. And I like it a little bit less.

Tuesday, 12th of July 2016

Today I chilled at home and continued watching my addictive series called Pablo Escobar on Netflix. It is about 73 episodes so it looks like until I finish it, I will be completely useless in my house of creativity.

But a little glance during breakfast got me looking at this article that emphasizes that parliament must decide whether it is good or bad for Britain to exit the EU.

This is exactly what I am talking about. It appears that politicians want to ignore this which makes me wonder if there is a hidden conspiracy. It is a bit like the war with Iraq when Tony Blair decided to ignore facts and public opinions and he went to war, and 9 years later a report confirms what people already knew way back then.

And in another article the little surprise came as Andrea Leadsom quits handing over the Prime Minister post to Theresa May.

She will be officially crowned the leader of the Conservative party tomorrow and the Prime Minister to take over from David Cameron.

Talk about being in the right place at the right time. I mean some people are destined to be what they are, for this woman hardly shed a tear nor sweated to get this prestigious position of Prime Minister.

Last year she would never have dreamt in a million years that she would ever be Prime Minister of Britain. Other people in her party and UKIP did all the dirty work, a woman MP died, and then other people got busted or chickened out. Well power to the Women and perhaps this has always been her destiny!

I later picked up the metro only for more surprises. Not only will Theresa May be the next Prime Minister of Britain but David Cameron is actually going to hand over to her today.

My heart beats so quickly and I read her statements that say 'Brexit will be Brexit'.

Another news is Angela Eagle is finally launching a challenge to Jeremy Corbyn's leadership. If you ask me, I don't think she has what it takes to be a strong leader for one simple reason. Why has it taken so long for her to launch this challenge finally when she had so much support behind her in the first place?

Anyway moving forward, David Cameron will have his last cabinet meeting and hand over to Theresa May.

It is so ironic that we thought we will have to wait until September or October 2016 for article 50 to be invoked but now we may not even have to wait until end of August 2016. I was speaking with a friend of mine yesterday and she was saying the EU Citizens in Britain still had 2 years and I told her 'no we didn't have that time because the whole Brexit process was going to be rushed', so let's wait and see.

Let's take an extract from this article and you will see there is little hope for EU citizens that have lived and worked in Britain for years.

http://www.msn.com/en-gb/news/uknews/theresa-may-vicars-daughter-unflappable/ar-BBucFwv?li=BBoPWjQ

> 'Theresa May, who will be 60 in October, suddenly finds herself poised to become Prime Minister two months earlier than she expected. She will have Cabinet appointments to make, favours to repay.'

I think that the fact that she has favours to repay in my mind says she is going to play the 'Brexit game' and take it all the way to the end.

http://www.independent.co.uk/voices/theresa-may-prime-minister-andrea-leadsom-policies-voting-record-human-rights-what-did-she-mean-a7130961.html

Wednesday, 13th of July 2016

The show must go on. Have you ever heard that popular saying and if you have not then at least you have heard the song by the British rock band Queen. 'The Show Must Go On' is a song which was the 12th and final track on their 1991 album Innuendo.

And basically with everything whatever the results, the show must go on. Today is Theresa May is Prime Minister and tomorrow it will be someone else again.

Well today the news is about financial shares that are falling in value in the crazy financial World. Also Ex-shadow cabinet minister Owen Smith is going to stand against Jeremy Corbyn. I think that this man may give Jeremy Corbyn a real ride for his money and not Angela Eagle. Tony Blair has criticised Jeremy Corbyn insisting that the labour party will be destroyed if he remains leader. I totally agree.

Thursday, 14th of July 2016

Well I woke up this morning and could not help smiling quietly when I read the British news. I must say this is the first time in the last 24 years that I have actually found British politics entertaining.

The first news, which came as a little bit of a surprise was that Theresa May had appointed Boris Johnson as the new Foreign Minister. I think this was a surprise for everyone around the World. And then finally the final piece of the puzzle came a bit later when I learnt that Michael Gove had been sacked. So the little show Boris put up to the media and public about being stabbed in the back was just him playing another one of his joker cards.

He must have known all along that he would be on Theresa's team. But the bit that everyone probably does not know is my personal analysis, is that he was scared to be a Prime Minister. Perhaps also scared for his life. So perhaps by handing the crown to Theresa, he hopes to contest this position later in the future when he has rebuilt his confidence.

But if my future analysis or shall I call it prediction is accurate, he is not destined for that great mighty post. When the time comes someone else will snatch his dream away right before his very eyes. In plain English from my perspective 'It is not Boris destiny to ever become the Prime Minister of England'.

Another piece of news that was interesting was a foreign policy spokesman for German Chancellor Angela Merkel's party was stating that so many suggestions coming from Britain about the Brexit are not workable. There was still the suggestion that Britain is still better off staying in the EU. Also George Osborne was sacked and replaced by Philip Hammond.

https://uk.news.yahoo.com/latest-german-official-uks-eu-082845334.html

The article below writes;

> "LONDON (Reuters) - Prominent pro-Brexit campaigner Michael Gove has been sacked from his cabinet post of justice secretary by Britain's new Prime Minister Theresa May, Sky
>
> (Reporting by Costas Pitas; editing by Michael Holden)"

https://uk.news.yahoo.com/pro-brexit-gove-sacked-british-government-sky-news-092300571--business.html

Friday, 15th of July 2016

I woke up today and the first news on most internet sites was about the terrorist that drove a truck into a crowd killing at least 84 people in France yesterday. The crowd in the seaside city of Nice on the French Riviera were celebrating Bastille Day, when this incident occurred.

My immediate thoughts are is this World is becoming more and more dangerous by day. It's really sad to be reading about the deaths of people almost every other day around the World.

Well this is Theresa May's newly formed cabinet.

Theresa May
WAS: Home Secretary
NOW: Prime Minister
Boris Johnson
WAS: Political Cabinet
NOW: Foreign Secretary
Liam Fox
WAS: Nothing
NOW: International Trade Secretary (new job)
David Davis
WAS: Nothing
NOW: Brexit Secretary (new job)
Damian Green
WAS: On the backbench
NOW: Work and Pensions Secretary
Andrea Leadsom
WAS: Energy minister (not Cabinet)
NOW: Environment Secretary
Gavin Williamson
WAS: Parliamentary Private Secretary
NOW: Chief Whip
James Brokenshire
WAS: Immigration Minister
NOW: Northern Ireland Secretary
Priti Patel
WAS: Employment Minister

NOW: Secretary of State for International Development

David Gauke

WAS: Financial Secretary to the Treasury (not Cabinet)

NOW: Chief Secretary to the Treasury

David Lidington

WAS: Europe Minister (not Cabinet)

NOW: Leader of the Commons

Baroness Evans of Bowes Park

WAS: Nothing

NOW: Leader of the House of Lords

Karen Bradley

WAS: Home Office minister (not Cabinet)

NOW: Culture Secretary

Ben Gummer

WAS: Home Office minister (not Cabinet)

NOW: Cabinet Office Minister

Philip Hammond

WAS: Foreign Secretary

NOW: Chancellor of the Exchequer

Amber Rudd

WAS: Energy and Climate Change Secretary

NOW: Home Secretary

Liz Truss

WAS: Environment Food & Rural Affairs Secretary

NOW: Justice Secretary

Justine Greening

WAS: International Development Secretary

NOW: Education Secretary and Minister for Women and Equalities

Chris Grayling

WAS: Leader of the House of Commons

NOW: Transport Secretary

Sajid Javid

WAS: Business Secretary

NOW: Secretary of State for Communities and Local Government

Greg Clark

WAS: Communities & Local Government Secretary

NOW: Secretary of State for Business, Energy and Industrial Strategy

Patrick McLoughlin

WAS: Transport Secretary

NOW: Conservative Party Chairman

Mark Harper

WAS: Chief Whip

NOW: Nothing

Michael Fallon

WAS: Defence Secretary

STILL: Defence Secretary

Jeremy Hunt

WAS: Health Secretary

STILL: Health Secretary

Alun Cairns

WAS: Welsh Secretary

STILL: Welsh Secretary

David Mundell

STILL: Scottish Secretary

Lord Taylor

STILL: Lords Chief Whip

Jeremy Wright

STILL: Attorney General

Monday, 18ᵗʰ of July 2016

Today's news is that Britain's Brexit minister said he wanted a generous settlement for Britons living in the EU and for Europeans in Britain after the country voted to leave the 28-nation bloc, but declined to fully guarantee the rights of EU citizens.

David Davis, who has said Britain should begin the formal process of leaving the EU by triggering Article 50 in early 2017, said on Sunday that the rights of EU citizens living in Britain should be agreed along with those of Britons in Europe. I agree but I think this should be done straightaway without before any negotiations begin.

https://uk.news.yahoo.com/brexit-minister-eu-citizens-arriving-uk-ahead-brexit-075850148--business.html

Tuesday, 19ᵗʰ of July 2016

Today I read that Angela Eagle has quit the labour leadership contest. I wonder why she entered it in the first place if she knew she wasn't going to put up a good fight.

Angela Eagle is quitting the race to challenge Jeremy Corbyn's leadership of the Labour party. So this means

Owen Smith is the only remaining contender to face Mr Corbyn.

https://uk.news.yahoo.com/angela-eagle-quits-labour-leadership-race-163200844.html

Wednesday, 20th of July 2016

Today's Brexit news is quite varied with a lot of exciting subjects. A few articles online focus on Nigel Farage. It appears his usage of his anti-migrant poster has been reported to the police. Some people are of the view that it incites hatred and racism.

The harm has been done so I am not sure anything fruitful will come out of this.

Another article says Nigel admits that the 'leave brexit' campaign pledge of giving the NHS the £350 million savings he forecasted was a mistake. Already it appears that alone swung a large number of votes towards the Brexit path. The harm is done and now we have to face what is next as this was an unfair advantage built on deception during the campaign for 'remain' or 'leave'. It is obvious that Nigel has got away with this questionable political tactic.

http://www.theguardian.com/politics/2016/jun/16/nigel-farage-defends-ukip-breaking-point-poster-queue-of-migrants

http://www.huffingtonpost.co.uk/entry/nigel-farage-good-morning-britain-eu-referendum-brexit-350-nhs_uk_576d0aa3e4b08d2c5638fc17

In the meantime the EU will not be pursuing their 6 month presidency of the European Council in 2017 as indicated by the new Prime Minister, Theresa May. The presidency rotates every 6 months and though it was the UK's turn, the Prime Minister will give it up so she can focus on preparing properly and carefully for the Brexit.

http://www.msn.com/en-gb/news/uknews/uk-will-not-take-on-eu-lead-role-says-pm/ar-BBuxUUG?li=BBoPWjQ

Another article talks about Hungarian budget airline Wizz Air. It was due to expand some services with the opportunity to provide more employment for the UK population before the Brexit. However because of the Brexit and the weaker pound it will not continue with this expansion plan.

https://uk.news.yahoo.com/wizz-air-cuts-uk-growth-093926282.html

Friday, 22nd of July 2016

So there are signs already even before the Brexit that there will be a serious impact on the British economy during and after the Brexit process. Already a few companies are delaying expansion plans and waiting to see what happens in 2017.

Another article shows that there has been an economic deterioration of the UK since people decided that they would leave the UK. Prices of food and other commodities will go up and future job cuts are to be expected with relocations of services to the other parts of the EU. It is in the best interest of the UK to try and get the access to the single market deal to ensure economic stability after the brexit.

https://uk.finance.yahoo.com/news/britain-just-got-first-concrete-084110488.html

Saturday, 23rd of July 23, 2016

Today is one of those days when there is hardly any news about the Brexit in the papers or on the internet. The main focus of the news is on other activities and events happening around the World.

People are beginning to absorb the shocking information about what Brexit actually means and it will take a few months to sink in since the prime Minister is not really going start the process until next year.

We can perhaps expect in the next couple of months a number of protests and perhaps court cases that are brexit related. The general atmosphere on the street is business as usual and everything is slowly coming back to normal as life goes on as usual.

Sunday, 24th of July 2016

Today is one of those quiet days again in the papers and the only news that is of relevance is one where the chairman of Britain's ruling Conservative Party, Patrick Mcloughlin, is speculating that the Brexit process is most likely to be initiated before the next general election.

https://uk.news.yahoo.com/conservative-party-chairman-says-brexit-binding-parliament-101758786.html?nhp=1

Monday, 25th of July 2016

(This World is going Crazy)

I have woken up with a thought in my head that the World is going crazy. We as a human race are developing so fast that we are no longer satisfied with calm and peace. We need constant drama and chaos in our lives to keep ourselves motivated. The current rumour is that EU members are becoming more united with the shocking result of the Brexit vote. They will be standing together united.

https://uk.finance.yahoo.com/news/europe-shrugging-off-shock-brexit-081154344.html

Another article explains Article 50 in detail and explains that during the negotiations there is actually a loophole in article 50 that allows Britain back into the EU if the negotiations are not successful. During the 2-year period, Britain can also change their mind and say we want to stay.

This is quite an interesting revelation and I wonder if the current UK government is fully aware of this possibility and the opportunities they may have in 2018 and 2019 to reverse the situation if there is a negative economic impact of brexit on the Country.

http://www.msn.com/en-gb/news/uknews/theres-a-loophole-in-article-50-that-lets-britain-back-into-the-eu-whenever-we-want/ar-BBuCmTZ

Thursday, 27th of July 2016

There has not been any relevant Brexit news for a while and I suppose this will be the situation until the beginning of next year. This is when the brexit show and drama will begin. Today I read a little bit more about triggering Article 50, which is the formal process for a country to exit the EU.

Apparently Giuliano Amato who is primarily responsible for writing this article, wrote it with clauses that would completely discourage countries from leaving the EU once they had joined. He made this claim in Rome recently. One of his sentences is 'When it comes to the economy they have to lose,' he said.

http://www.msn.com/en-gb/news/world/article-50-was-never-supposed-to-be-used-says-the-man-who-wrote-it/ar-BBuTgJh?li=BBoPWjQ

August 2016

Thursday, 25th of August 2016

It has been a while since I entered any news into this Brexit diary. The sea is calm at the moment. Not much has being going on and it will probably be this way until later in the year.

Many EU citizens are now trying to seek UK citizenship which can be a log process. First you have to apply for residence permit, then you need to take the UK life test and finally you have to pay around £1300 along with an application to the Home office, if you pass through all those hurdles.

The article below talks about the number of EU nationals seeking citizenship that has gone up since this Brexit, and many people are very disappointed that the UK government is not guaranteeing the rights of EU citizens in the UK.

https://uk.news.yahoo.com/brexit-sparks-uk-citizenship-stampede-among-eastern-europeans-184700512.html

Another article below also highlights the same issue. Most EU citizens are worried about their future in the UK and would be applying at least for residence permit. The article is titled 'Brexit Triggers Stampede For UK Citizenship'.

http://www.msn.com/en-gb/news/uknews/brexit-triggers-stampede-for-uk-citizenship/ar-BBw0Q3H?li=BBoPWjQ&ocid=mailsignout

September 2016

Sunday, 11th of September 2016

The month of August and September has been very quiet for everyone in terms of Brexit news. The Labour party and all its drama again is making more headline news.

Another article talks about Boris Johnson trying to put pressure on the government to deliver on the referendum result. This is really ironic coming from someone who disappeared briefly from the scene, when 17 million voters needed him and believed in him. He has been given a second chance by the Theresa May, and now he wants people to look at him again as if he has the answers and solution that the country is looking for.

https://uk.news.yahoo.com/boris-johnson-makes-change-britain-plea-no-10-002100596.html

October 2016

Wednesday, 5th October 2016

Gradually this month Brexit news is beginning to pick up. The latest articles today focus on a proposal by the new UK Home Secretary Amber Rudd that companies need to compile a list of all foreign workers. This proposal has been met with great disappointment by a large number of people. Someone even compared it to the time of the Nazi party in the 1930.

I find the proposal also very intimidating. According to Amber Rudd's proposal, this is intended to prevent 'migrants taking jobs that British people can do'.

There are so many jobs that British people can do but historically have been known not to do them that has made it easier for foreign migrants to do these roles. We are talking about many fields like the health sector and farming industry. See article below for more information.

https://uk.yahoo.com/news/mps-britain-cant-believe-government-wants-draw-list-073119197.html

And another piece of hilarious political news is the Nigel Farage is back as the UKIP leader just as Diane James quits with only 18 days in the job.

http://www.bbc.co.uk/news/uk-politics-37561065

Thursday, 13ᵗʰ of October 2016

Today is an interesting court day. It appears that we have some Brexit demonstrators protesting outside the High Court. There is a legal challenge that has been brought on by some people to force the British government to pursue parliamentary approval before triggering Article 50, which begins the formal process of leaving the European Union. It is very unclear whether this will have any significant bearing on the outcome of the referendum but it is still interesting to follow.

https://uk.news.yahoo.com/legal-challenge-uk-governments-trigger-brexit-begins-092825275--sector.html

Tuesday, 25th of October 2016

Another Brexit blow to the UK government is Australia cannot agree a free-trade deal with Britain until they have left the EU.

Steven Ciobo, Australia's trade minister cannot even enter formal talks as this will be illegal. Therefore it appears exploring a lucrative free-trade deal with Australia is out of the window until the later part of 2019 if everything goes according to Theresa's Brexit plan.

More can be read in the article below.

http://www.msn.com/en-gb/money/news/australia-has-just-dealt-a-massive-blow-to-the-uk-governments-brexit-plans/ar-AAjmFQm?li=BBoPOOl&ocid=mailsignout

Wednesday, 29ᵗʰ October 2016

And as we get towards the end of October an exciting development is happening in Northern Ireland. The extract from the news reads as follows;

'Northern Ireland's High Court on Friday rejected an attempt to block Britain's exit from the European Union, saying that neither the province's parliament nor its laws could override a decision by the British government. But it said it would defer to English courts on the wider issue of whether the British government has the right to invoke Article 50 of the EU Lisbon Treaty to leave the bloc without the explicit backing of the British parliament. Prime Minister Theresa May welcomed the ruling, with a spokesman saying it would allow the British government "to proceed to trigger Article 50 as planned.'

http://uk.reuters.com/article/uk-britain-eu-nireland-idUKKCN12S11U

November 2016

Monday, 3rd of November 2016

(Interesting Court ruling)

There is an interesting court ruling in the British courts today that is causing pandemonium and surprise across the country. The courts have agreed with business woman, Gina Miller, that the new Prime Minister, Theresa May, cannot trigger Article 50 without parliamentary approval.

This is quite positive from the courts as the message it sends out to people is that our democratic system works. The government intend to appeal this decision but for now we can all believe that democracy still exists in Great Britain because I was beginning to lose faith in it.

https://uk.yahoo.com/news/may-cannot-trigger-brexit-government-loses-high-court-101300161.html

A lot of people after today's court ruling will be wondering who is Gina Miller? I mean she has just won a battle against the government. Many newspaper articles are analysing her and digging into her background.

Read more about her and todays court ruling read the 2 links below.

http://www.ibtimes.co.uk/who-gina-miller-businesswoman-won-appeal-against-government-triggering-article-50-1589704

http://www.bbc.co.uk/news/uk-politics-37857785

Apparently there was a rumour that Article 50 was going to be invoked by mid-January 2017. The March 2017 date was meant to be a decoy, so this action by the court today has certainly halted any possible unprofessional act of an unexpected surprise in the New Year.

http://www.bbc.co.uk/news/uk-politics-37857785

Friday, 4th November 2016

Everyone is still recovering from the shock brexit government defeat. But today it appears our new Prime Minister, Theresa may, has come bouncing back. Perhaps there were quick discussions last night of options and possibilities and backup plans because this morning she is extremely confident that she will win the appeal in Court.

Theresa may is extremely confident that she will meet her March 2017 deadline.

I wonder why she is that confident. That makes me think there is a backup plan even if she loses

http://www.independent.co.uk/news/uk/politics/brexit-theresa-may-is-confident-of-victory-in-supreme-court-over-article-50-a7397356.html

Thursday, 17th November 2016

This month is also very quiet with regards to Brexit news. Everyone is waiting for the appeal case to begin in December. This is where the government will try to overturn the court's decision that Theresa may cannot trigger Article 50 without parliamentary approval.

In the meantime there is an article that says that the UK will face £100bn budget black hole in the next 5 years and Brexit is to blame for it. Please read link below.

https://uk.news.yahoo.com/brexit-blamed-uks-100bn-budget-black-hole-022800854.html

Friday, 18th November 2016

Another interesting article today concerns Scotland and Wales.

The article is titled' Scottish and Welsh governments can intervene in Brexit court case'. It states that both the Scottish and Welsh government will be permitted to interfere in the court regarding how the Brexit process should be triggered in the United Kingdom. Again I don't think this has any kind of impact on the Brexit process.

https://uk.yahoo.com/news/scottish-welsh-governments-intervene-brexit-court-case-121800029.html

December 2016

Monday, 5th of December 2016

This is the last month of the year. I call it the Christmas month. It was not long ago on the 23rd of June when 17 million people in Britain decided that they want to leave the EU during the Brexit referendum. And on the 13th of July we had history as Theresa May was sworn in as the Prime Minister of the UK. She became the second woman in the Country to hold this prestigious political position.

One of her key messages was that 'Brexit is Brexit' and she will be pursuing it all the way. If I have to interpret that, then that means a hard Brexit because the UK will not have access to the single market if it does not accept the terms and conditions that come with it as imposed by the EU.

But what is interesting about today, is the case of Gina Miller against the government is being brought to court today. 11 of UK's senior judges will listen to debates from both sides and decide if the government needs parliament approval before triggering article 50) which starts the formal process for leaving the EU. They will debate all day today and resume tomorrow.

https://www.theguardian.com/politics/live/2016/dec/05/brexit-article-50-supreme-court-hearing-live-updates

Wednesday, 7th of December 2016

Today as usual is quiet regarding Brexit news. The supreme courts are still debating and no date has been set for the final judgement of Gina versus the Government. There is some speculation that the judgement will most likely be in the New Year.

In the meant time there is an article which writes that Theresa May will publish her Brexit plan before triggering Article 50. It will be interesting to see what that plan entails and how detailed it is.

http://www.msn.com/en-gb/news/uknews/may-says-she-will-reveal-brexit-plan-before-triggering-article-50/ar-AAlevlE?li=BBoPRmx&ocid=mailsignout

Thursday, 8th of December 2016

Today the Brexit court case has ended and we will have to wait for the outcome probably in the first or second week of 2017.

In the meantime in England MPs have already carried out a vote which supports Theresa May's timetable of beginning the formal process of leaving the EU latest by March 2017. The votes were 448 – 75 which means that there was a clear majority of 373.

However keys questions regarding the single market and migration probably still need to be made clear before Article 50 is triggered.

https://uk.yahoo.com/news/mps-vote-back-government-timetable-article-50-192700139.html

Wednesday, 14th of December 2016

The final brexit of the year has set in as we wait for results of the court case. And believe you me when I say next year is going to be an exciting year. Full of Brexit action.

A lot of things have happened this year since the results of the Brexit referendum. Jobs have been lost, the pound has fallen and even Lego has pushed up its prices in the UK due to the Brexit.

There is even an article where Helena Kennedy QC, the Chair of the House of Lords advises the EU citizens to start compiling paperwork which shows how long they have lived and worked in the United Kingdom.

This is essential for applying for the residence permit and also essential for applying for naturalisation, if you are an EU citizen.

https://www.theguardian.com/politics/2016/dec/14/eu-citizens-collect-proof-of-living-in-uk-helena-kenney-qc-lords-brexit-reports

Thursday, 15th December 2016

The news in Brussels today regarding Brexit is that there is a division amongst members on the negotiating tactics to be used for the Brexit process with UK. The article is titled 'EU leaders turn on each other over Brexit negotiation tactics'.

I think this is normal. We have 27 members and each has an idea of how they would want to negotiate the exiting terms for Britain. But it will all come together eventually.

There is a suggestion that the European Commission, led by Jean-Claude Juncker wants Britain to pay a divorce bill of about 60 billion euros before any talks over the future EU-UK trade relationship commence.

I think rules are rules and if there is a price to pay for leaving the EU then Britain should pay as this was made clear before they became members of the EU in 1973. I can definitely see it from Jean-Claude Juncker's point of view. You need to play by the rules in other to be treated fairly or favourably.

http://www.msn.com/en-gb/news/world/eu-leaders-turn-on-each-other-over-brexit-negotiation-tactics/ar-AAlzfcj?li=BBoPWjQ&ocid=mailsignout

Saturday, 24th of December 2016

(Today is Christmas Eve.)

An amusing Brexit article today suggests that government is also keeping the Brexit plans from the Queen and she is getting frustrated. So it appears that not only are the public in the dark regarding Brexit but also the Queen. And all the 3 million EU citizens are also uncertain about their future at the moment in England.

https://uk.news.yahoo.com/government-even-keeping-brexit-strategy-113742649.html

And today the Prime Minister has made a speech and she is asking for the country to unite and be stronger. She has talked about great divisions happening during and after the EU referendum, and she has asked people to come together and move forward in her Christmas message.

https://uk.yahoo.com/news/british-pm-urges-post-brexit-vote-unity-2017-051346233.html

Sunday, 25th of December 2016

(Today is Christmas day.)

And today is a day for celebration as we celebrate Christmas. But today for many EU citizens that celebration will be short with cautiousness as no one knows what the future holds for the 3 million EU citizens living and working in the UK at the moment.

People are applying for residential permits in thousands and there is even an article that suggests that many banks and financial organisations are considering moving to Ireland.

I am sure that individuals and business will be looking to relocate to countries all within the EU. Even individuals that are certain about their status may still consider moving to other parts of Europe.

https://www.theguardian.com/world/2016/dec/25/uk-banks-financial-firms-moving-ireland

Wednesday, 28th of December 2016

Today is a special day as I will close the entries for this month today with the final Brexit news of the year.

There is an interesting article explaining what we have signed up for and what the present UK government are not admitting to us in public.

In quotes it writes 'Theresa May 'lacks courage to admit complexity of Brexit' and goes on further to explain 'Whitehall union leader says civil service will need more resources or government will have to change its priorities'.

I think this says it all. The March 2017 deadline is rushing the United Kingdom into a process that has not been fully prepared for at all. What we are going to experience once we begin post-brexit talks with the UK, is pressure and many areas in the civil service will be under-resourced to deal with issues that arise from the Brexit process. Areas like housing, migration and even the economy will feel this pressure.

Just imagine all these new properties being built all around the country, when businesses and individuals are planning to relocate elsewhere in Europe, since there may be no more single market and freedom of movement. Are people going to buy property or put it on hold between late 2017 and 2019? How can people afford things when prices go up and there is the possibility of mass job cuts across the country?

We have so many schools and colleges. How will Brexit affect funding for the education sector which has already seen massive cuts in the last few years?

There are so many unanswered questions at the moment and the government is not exposing the real challenges we will be facing to us at the moment.

https://www.theguardian.com/politics/2016/dec/28/ministers-lack-courage-to-admit-complexity-of-brexit-say-civil-servants

January 2017

Tuesday, 3rd of January 2017

The New Year 2017, has begun and the 2017 Brexit news has just started to slowly take off the ground.

Today there is talk of Britain's EU ambassador who has suddenly quit, just months before the Brexit negotiations occur.

I don't think this has any real significance on the Brexit process. Sir Ivan, was appointed in his role by David Cameron in 2013. I really didn't even know who he was until I read about him in the papers today so I personally will not be missing him although Brussels might.

Friday, 6th of January 2017

I know the reality of the Brexit vote has not yet hit majority of the British population but some impact can already be felt. Jamie Oliver is apparently going to shut 6 of his Italian restaurants around the country and he is blaming the Brexit for his actions. Significant jobs will be lost at his restaurants and this is all linked with the Brexit. There are more job cuts to come, once Article 50 is triggered I think. Everyone across the country will feel the economic job crunch after Theresa May has triggered Article 50 in March 2017.

Monday, 9th January 2017

Today I read the news that the value of the pound has fallen to a two-month low against major currencies after Prime Minister Theresa May indicated that the UK would follow up with a 'hard Brexit' from the EU.

By a hard Brexit, Theresa May, means no flexibility with negotiations. This affects EU citizens tremendously as many of the 3 million EUs living and working in the United Kingdom will be uncertain of their future. Some will already be making long term plans to leave this country. Many businesses may also make that decision to move elsewhere in Europe which will have a log-term effect on the economy of Britain.

People and business really need re-assurances quickly or they will not wait and this can have a long-term negative effect on the economy.

Tuesday, 10th of January 2017

The news of the Brexit is sluggish at the moment as the entire country is waiting for the Supreme Court to decide whether the government needs approval from parliament before it can trigger Article 50.

Gina Millar the business woman who was the main person amongst a number of parties to bring this case to court has already made a lot of enemies and friends across Britain. She has become dangerously famous over-night in the UK. If she wins then there may be a slight delay as Theresa May will need parliament's approval before she can trigger article 50.

No official date has been set for the highest court's judgment but it is expected to be at some point in January 2017.

Wednesday, 11th of January 2017

I read an article that there was a suggestion that £1000 is to be charged for anyone hiring an EU worker. Now this is whole thing is getting out of hand. Apparently Immigration Minister, Robert Goodwill exposed the plans in a House of Lords subcommittee gathering. The idea is that for every EU worker employed, an employer will have to pay £1000 a year. This currently applies to non-

EU workers. Later in the evening the idea was dismissed as ridiculous a few others in the Country.

Tuesday, 17th January 2017

Today is the long awaited speech by Theresa May on the Brexit. At around 15.02pm, I read parts of the speech and sighed. The woman wants a hard Brexit and has verbally indicated that Britain will not be part of the European Single Market. She explained that the parliament will vote on the final package that she is deciding this with her close allies.

12 main points of Theresa Mays speech concerning Brexit

1. Certainty
2. Control of our own laws
3. Strengthen the Union
4. Maintain the Common Travel Area with Ireland
5. Control of immigration
6. Rights for EU nationals in Britain, and British nationals in the EU
7. Protect workers' rights
8. Free trade with European markets
9. New trade agreements with other countries
10. The best place for science and innovation
11. Cooperation in the fight against crime and terrorism
12. A smooth, orderly Brexit

After analysing her speech I must say it is a very good speech on paper but workers' rights are already protected. Anyone who has lived and worked in the UK for many years should automatically be protected.

Also on point 10., we need to be realistic and understand that science and innovation requires investment. A politician's words do not guarantee that essential funding, that is required to promote science and innovation nationally.

The EU has made Britain a great place for innovation and scientific research through generous funding over the years. We can see this funding happening in places like London and Liverpool where there has been a lot of research and innovation. This funding will cease in the next coming years and have a serious impact on research across the UK.

New trade agreements have been happening for years but the issue is what kind of impact will the new trade deals have? Will the new trade deals secure millions jobs or just benefit a few hundred people? And finally the idea of free trade when Britain has very little to offer to the EU after the Brexit is very ambitious. Education and accommodation is over-priced. There will be no more free capital and movement of people so why would European countries be interested in doing business with Britain in the future? Think about it.

For the full article of the PMs Speech, you can read the link below.

http://www.independent.co.uk/news/uk/home-news/full-text-theresa-may-brexit-speech-global-britain-eu-european-union-latest-a7531361.html

So many companies and businesses are already hinting that they will be relocating their businesses to other parts of Europe. See article below;

https://uk.yahoo.com/news/pm-single-market-announcement-threatens-134855342.html

The key message in this article states that 'But Len McCluskey, general secretary of Britain's biggest trade union Unite, said the Prime Minister's stance put future investment in industries such as car manufacturing in the UK in jeopardy.'

Last year, SMMT boss Mike Hawes also hinted that the UK's car manufacturing industry risked lots of job losses once Brexit is pursued.

The pound has also collapsed today to $1.1986, which is its lowest since October's when it was sent to a 31-year low of $1.1841.

So here we go as the countdown begins now as our days are numbered before the trigger for article 50 is pushed.

Wednesday, 18th January 2017

After Prime Minister Theresa May acknowledged that any Brexit deal would be put to parliamentary vote yesterday, it appears the pound has improved slightly to $1.23.

Today almost every media has a story reacting to Theresa Mays speech last night.

A very interesting article I read is shown below and I took a little extract from the web link.

'The European Parliament's chief Brexit negotiator has criticised Theresa May's "threatening" tactics and warned the days of Britain cherry-picking its relationship with Brussels are over.

Guy Verhofstadt said the Prime Minister's decision to suggest the UK would become a low-tax, low-regulation haven if the EU failed to agree a good exit deal was a "counter-productive" strategy.'

http://www.msn.com/en-gb/news/uknews/theresa-may-slammed-by-brexit-negotiator-over-threatening-tactics/ar-AAlXi1b?li=BBoPRmx&ocid=mailsignout

Thursday, 19th of January 2017

So there are huge jobs shifts planning to occur very quickly once Article 50, is triggered according to an article I read today.

HSBC may plan to shift at least 1,000 jobs each from UK. Also 2 of Europe's biggest banks also warned that they could each move about 1,000 jobs out of London elsewhere in Europe.

HSBC Chief Executive Stuart Gulliver indicated a relocation of staff to Paris. UBS Chairman Axel Weber indicated that about 1000 of its staff could also be affected.

Finally Germany's Handelsblatt newspaper also stated that Goldman Sachs may consider moving some of its operations once Brexit is triggered.

Friday, 20th of January 2017

Today I read that although Theresa May's speech sounds convincing, her main problem is that she only has 2 years to achieve her Brexit plan once she starts the Brexit process formally in March 2017.

Lots of changes will slowly impact the economy of Britain as food prices rise, massive job cuts happen across the country. Also large-scale reduction of public funding will happen across the country over the next 2 – 5 years that will affect rural and urban development.

Another article talks about the labour leader, Jeremy Corbyn. It appears he is softening on his approach to force his MPs to vote in favour of triggering Article 50. To be honest I am not sure why one man should have the power to force his

MPs to vote in a certain way. I thought that this was a democratic society and not a dictatorship.

Monday, 23rd of January 2017

Today is a very important day as the Supreme Court judges are to decide on a verdict on Theresa May's plans for EU withdrawal tomorrow. Everyone is anxious as they will decide tomorrow whether Theresa May has the authority to withdraw the UK from the European Union without the consent of the parliament.

Just a reminder, this case was brought against the government by a number of parties and Gina Miller, who is a philanthropist and former investment banker is the leading person. The case first went to the High Court in November 2016 where she won. The government appealed the verdict, and the case was referred to the Supreme Court in December 2016.

Tuesday, 24th of January 2017

Well Gina Miller has won but her victory and celebration will be very short as the UK government already has a backup plan set into almost immediate motion. The Supreme Court judges have said Parliament approval is required before Theresa May can trigger Article 50 which starts the 2 year formal Brexit process. The ruling of the Supreme Judges on this matter was 8-3.

The government will now bring a bill to parliament which they apparently have ready. There is already a talk of a fast track bill that the government will put forward to parliament in just a few days.

The historical news today demonstrates that a Prime Minister needs the votes of the MPs before it can trigger Article 50 when making major decisions that affect the whole of the United Kingdom.

Wednesday, 25th of January 2017

Today the papers and media are plastered with the news of the Supreme Judges' verdict. Gina Miller has already become a hated figure, and a man was arrested for apparent racial abuse of Gina Miller as reported by Sky news online.

In the meantime the countdown begins for Article 50 to be triggered. It is almost as if yesterday's court verdict was just some form of formality and has no bearing on the overall Brexit process.

Labour MPS are being told to vote in favour of anything that Theresa May puts across the table.

When you take your mind back to the beginning you can now put the puzzle together and see that Jeremy Corbyn was just a Brexit puppet and he is trying to turn his MPs into Brexit puppets as well.

So it will be interesting to see what happens when the government puts a bill across to Parliament which I understand is already prepared and can happen at any time.

Once a majority of MPs vote 'yes', then we can round up the number of days, when in March 2017, Article 50 will be triggered.

In the meantime the only woman (Gina Miller) in the country apart from Scottish First Minister (Nicola Sturgeon), who has genuinely fought in favour of a fair and democratic process, is being abused and threatened all around the internet and in real life.

The general atmosphere around the country is quiet. People have given up and most EU citizens are waiting and are prepared for the worst. EU citizens who have a backup plan have implemented it. I feel like we are in storm and this is the calming part. It is like watching the waves of tsunami from afar and thinking it is just a mild wave, and even when it is drawing nearer to the land it is still not taken seriously

Another interesting article is about a British lawyer who wants to ask the Irish Courts whether they can do a U-turn on Brexit. I mean is this a joke. Last minute protest! - Where was this man last year June and July 2016, when thousands of EU and UK citizens were lamenting in street protests all over the country? Is he trying to get some cheap publicity for himself?

Please refer to article below.

http://www.msn.com/en-gb/money/topstories/a-british-lawyer-wants-the-irish-courts-to-ask-if-theres-a-way-back-from-brexit/ar-AAlQmu6?ocid=mailsignout

Thursday, 26th January 2017

Today Theresa May's government has published the bill that will begin the process of pulling Britain out of the EU. The bill once approved will be the key to triggering Article 50. Apparently there has been a limited amount of days given to MPs to debate the bill which amounts up to 5 working days.

The bill is about 137 words long and it will be scrutinised in the House of Commons. Already Labour leader wants to force his MPs to support the bill.

The main concerns about the bill at the moment are protection of workers' rights and securing 'full tariff- and impediment-free access' to the EU's single market.

This is just a formality that Theresa May has to go through as she is still on target to trigger Article 50 by the end of March 2017.

Sunday, 29th of January 2017

Today things have quietened down and the only Brexit show is the much awaited debate about the bill that will be debated by the House of Commons and the House of Lords.

There are rumours that some British citizens in Germany are trying to apply for German citizenship and the reverse is happening also in the United Kingdom. No one is sure of the future and where ever possible both individuals and businesses want to take precaution.

There is also news about some supporters that are revolting against the labour leader, Jeremy Corbyn.

February 2017

Wednesday, 1st of February 2017

Today is a very special day in terms of Brexit news. By this evening, the Prime Minister Theresa May will know if MPs in the House of Commons will vote in favour of her to take the Country out of the EU. If they vote against her then her Brexit Bill will go to the House of Lords for voting. What is interesting about this Brexit Bill is that it is only 137 words long.

137 words, I mean is this a joke. I have not read this but just the number of words alone tells me that this was just quickly scribbled down by someone. In the meantime the voting is to happen around 7.00pm. The Brexit Bill has been debated in Parliament for 2 days prior to this vote.

http://www.liverpoolecho.co.uk/news/liverpool-news/brexit-everything-you-need-know-12538404

Thursday, 2nd of February 2017

Today I read that there are three more cases going to court which may slow down Brexit. I personally think that this article is slightly over –exaggerating the delay. The 3 cases are the EEA case, the Dublin Case and the expat's case. Read more about these cases in the link below.

https://uk.news.yahoo.com/three-more-court-cases-seeking-disrupt-brexit-094200407.html

Wednesday, 8th of February 2017

Well we are getting to the final Brexit Hurdle. Today the MPs will be voting for the last time on the Brexit Bill in the House of Commons. Just a few days ago on the 2nd of February 2017, MPs voted to authorise the Prime Minister to commence the Article 50 talks with the EU. Today after 3 days of debate on the Brexit Bill, the MPs in the House of Commons will be voting for the final time on this Bill.

https://www.thesun.co.uk/news/2755385/brexit-bill-theresa-may-article-50-vote/

Friday, 10th of February 2017

I read that about Michel Barnier today. He is currently the EU Brexit negotiator. According to web article, it writes that Michel will be demanding that UK pays £48bn as its divorce bill.

That is a lot of money to pay and I wonder if that has been fully taken into consideration by the new Prime Minister. What is the impact of refusing to pay the bill? Will Britain continue to receive all its EU funding if it decides to pay this Bill. These are the kind of questions I will be pondering on if I am the government.

Will there be any negotiations at all if Britain refuses to pay? I think Britain wants to play by the rules, it should agree payment.

https://uk.yahoo.com/news/brexit-negotiator-michel-barnier-set-demand-uk-pays-053900440.html

Friday, 17th of February 2017

I woke up today and the name 'Tony Blair' made the Brexit news for the day. Apparently after nearly a year of complete silence, he has come out to encourage the public to change their minds on the Brexit result.

I find this a huge surprise as why leave a fight until the last minute? It is like being battered black and blue in a boxing ring and waiting till the last minute of the last round to hopefully deliver a knock-out blow for victory.

According to the article it quotes 'Tony Blair has waded back into British politics by urging the public to "rise up" and change their mind on Brexit if Theresa May tries to quit the EU "at any cost".'

There is also another interesting quote which in which he says 'that voters are more worried about non-European migrants -who are 'from different cultures' and pose a 'security threat' - rather than EU citizens who more easily integrate into British communities.'

To be perfectly honest his opinion could be accurate but it is not relevant anymore as the fight has been left when it his voice is no longer effective.

Article 50 is going to be triggered in March 2017, just next month and I personally believe it is too late to start bringing forward debates or arguments.

http://www.huffingtonpost.co.uk/entry/tony-blair-brexit-at-any-cost-no-eu-migration-bloomberg-imperfect-knowledge-cliff-edge-change-mind_uk_58a61f32e4b045cd34bff43d

https://uk.yahoo.com/news/tony-blair-tells-remainers-rise-denies-responsibility-brexit-104700101.html

Monday, 20th of February 2017

Today news talks about the faith of 4.2 million EU citizens. The number seems to be increasing as I thought we only had 3 million EU citizens in the UK. The House of Lords wants the government to provide assurance to the EU citizens that are currently working and living in the UK. But the current government only wants to give verbal assurance.

http://money.cnn.com/2017/02/20/news/economy/uk-migrants-eu-brexit/index.html

Meanwhile, there has been a protest by masses of people in a campaign called 'One Day Without Us'. The campaign objective is to highlight the contribution migrants make to the U.K.

Tuesday, 21st of February 2017

The only Brexit news I can find today is about what the cost of leaving the EU will be for Britain. The article suggests that Europe wants Britain to continue to pay lots of money amounting to billions into EU schemes until 2023. The idea is that a bill of £60 billion is settled this way by Britain.

I don't know how authentic this claim is but I can see some positives from this. It means that many schemes we have in the UK will not just suddenly dry up of funds. So many areas in the country including Liverpool and Blackpool have been developed with EU money. Research in the UK has been progressing with EU money. Imagine the devastating effect all these multiple areas around the country will face when their funds are suddenly cut.

http://www.msn.com/en-gb/news/uknews/europe-wants-britain-to-pay-billions-into-eu-schemes-up-until-2023/ar-AAn8Zur?li=BBoPWjQ&ocid=iehp

Wednesday, 22nd of February 2017

The papers today write about Brexit Secretary David Davis. Apparently he insists that we will still need EU migrants for many years to come. Many jobs are not appealing to the British public and therefore EU migrants will still be required for these jobs.

http://www.msn.com/en-gb/money/news/we-will-need-eu-migrants-for-years-admits-davis/ar-AAncHVo?li=BBoPWjQ&ocid=mailsignout

Another article writes about the lowest drop in the number of EU workers has occurred since the Brexit vote. This data is recorded by the Office of National Statistics (ONS).

http://www.msn.com/en-gb/money/markets/britain-sees-largest-drop-in-eu-workers-for-5-years-fueling-fears-of-a-labor-shortage/ar-AAn0FNx

Thursday, 23rd of February 2017

The brexit news today focuses on low numbers of net-migration. It seems there are fewer international students coming into the country in the last 12 months compared to the year before. Some people are attributing this to the Brexit vote. I think that could be partly responsible. Higher cost of living, high tuition fees and uncertainty about the future will reduce net-migration but it will also have an adverse effect on the economy because it also means reduction of income.

https://www.theguardian.com/uk-news/2017/feb/23/net-migration-to-uk-falls-by-49000-after-brexit-vote

Friday, 24th of February 2017

There is nothing new in the news today about Brexit. There is however focus on the Labour party about Jeremy Corbyn who claims he is not responsible for a Labour's by-election defeat in Copeland.

I find it strange that he does not realise that he has contributed to this result just by simply being the labour leader, and there will be more results like this as Labour is perceived by many as a weak party. I don't think many people are compatible with his personality and hence he is not popular. I therefore personally think, Labour need a change in leadership very quickly to avoid further surprise defeats.

https://www.theguardian.com/politics/2017/feb/24/jeremy-corbyn-labour-leader-brexit-uk-political-landscape-copeland-byelection

Saturday, 25th of February 2017

Today a website writes an interesting article which claims that as soon as Theresa May triggers Article 50, she will immediately end the right of EU citizens' rights to live in the UK. It claims this is because the government is afraid of a large number of Bulgarians and Romanians coming in the last 2 years of the post-Brexit talks.

I find this quite scary for everyone including EU citizens that have a right to live and work in the UK. Once she triggers Article 50, just imagine the nightmare every EU citizen would have when travelling abroad or for a weekend away in Europe and trying to re-enter the UK. I can just foresee many pathetic and sad stories coming forward from December 2017 onwards. I think all EU nationals need to ensure that they at least apply for residence permit before they set out travelling for holidays or business outside the UK once Article 50 is triggered.

http://www.msn.com/en-gb/news/uknews/may-to-end-eu-citizens%e2%80%99-rights-to-live-permanently-in-uk-within-days-over-fear-%e2%80%98half-of-romania-and-bulgaria%e2%80%99-will-come/ar-AAntD6O?li=BBoPWjQ&ocid=iehp

Tuesday, 28th of February 2017

The news today is about BMW. It is considering moving some of their services to Germany from Oxford. I think once the formal Brexit talks begin with the EU, we are going to be hearing more stories about businesses moving their operation to other parts of Europe.

The main reason why business and companies will be moving is because of a hard Brexit and the lower pound. This will seriously affect the economy of England.

https://uk.yahoo.com/finance/news/brexit-bmw-considers-moving-production-081708354.html

Today Theresa May is expected to lose her Brexit Bill vote in the House of Lords. Although it has passed through the House of Commons, the House of Lords still need to agree the vote. Right now the argument is about the fate of the EU citizens that are living in the UK and have worked here for years.

The article below quotes 'The Government is accused of using EU citizens as bargaining chips'. The article goes on further to write 'Lords wanted a clause in Ms May's bill to trigger Article 50 stating that EU citizens already in the UK will have the same rights to live and work here after Brexit.'

I think this should be automatic. I mean we live in a democratic society and I support the House of Lords decision.

Please read the link below for more information.

http://www.independent.co.uk/news/uk/politics/brexit-latest-eu-citizens-rights-theresa-may-amber-rudd-house-of-lords-a7604566.html

March 2017

Wednesday, 1st of March 2017

There are rumours that the Brexit bill will be defeated by the Lords today. The reason why it will be defeated is because of the rights of EU citizens already living and working in the United Kingdom.

https://uk.yahoo.com/news/brexit-bill-defeated-lords-over-eu-nationals-rights-194800780.html

Another news making headlines is a statement by the former Prime Minister, John Mayor. He apparently saying that 'brexit voters made a historic mistake' and the voters are naïve.'

I have to agree with him because the 17 million voters probably did not analyse very far into the future when they voted 'Brexit'. But for now the harm is done and there is no use crying over spilled milk they say.

http://news.sky.com/story/major-brexit-voters-made-a-historic-mistake-10784495

Thursday, 2nd of March 2017

So the vote happened and the Government had a taste of its first defeat over the Brexit bill. The vote was 358 to 256 and it supported the amendment of protecting the rights of the EU citizens in the UK post-Brexit era. Despite the defeat the government is confident that they will still trigger Article 50 latest by the end of March 2017. It is speculated the bill will be taken to the House of Commons for voting either on the 13th or 14th of March 2017.

https://uk.yahoo.com/news/govt-confident-meeting-brexit-deadline-despite-lords-defeat-040700696.html

So the Brexit time is ticking 'tick, tick' and here we are in the final moments before Article 50 is triggered and there is utter Brexit pandemonium this morning. All major news carry the same Brexit story packaged with different wrappings.

I think it is very cruel to use vulnerable people as bargaining chips. Theresa is adamant that she wants to start Brexit negotiations in time within her March 2017 timetable. I am not sure why she is in such a hurry when there is no reason to be.

Whether Article 50 is triggered today or next year or never, life still goes on and one day in the future this whole Brexit topic will be history, and a new topic or issue will take its place.

But for now EU citizens can breathe a sigh of relief as there are other people and politicians who have a moral obligation towards humanity.

One more article talks about what if both the House of Commons and the House of Lords disagree on the Brexit Bill? Then what will happen? Will it be a game of Ping-Pong table tennis? Well I don't think it can last that long because the longest UK political Ping-Pong game occurred in 2005 and it lasted only 36 hours. This was during the passage of Tony Blair's 2005 Prevention of Terrorism bill.

Friday, 3rd of March 2017

Right now the two English Queens of Brexit are at battle. Nicola Sturgeon the First Minister of Scotland is calling for a second referendum for Scotland and, Theresa May (PM) is saying that now is not the time. The media is full of coverage of the feud between these two women.

See article below for more information.

https://uk.yahoo.com/news/theresa-may-warn-snp-stop-playing-politics-over-225200852.html

Sunday, 5th of March 2017

The story today in the media is a familiar one. The main familiar concern is the call for Theresa May to guarantee the rights of EU citizens after the Brexit. The same concern is for British people who are living in other parts of Europe. I feel this should be guaranteed for everyone and it should not even be up for negotiation.

What most people don't realise is until you are affected you will not understand the devastating effect that this can have on an individual, family and friends. If you have lived all your life, or most part of your life in a country, and you are one day shipped to a strange land, just imagine how that can affect an individual mentally and emotionally. And think about the long-term effect on family, friends and loved ones that no longer have access to the individual.

I still don't understand how a partner can vote to leave and the other vote to remain. For me that shows no respect and love between a couple, and I heard of cases where wives, husbands and partners voted differently from the other during the EU referendum. It just indicates to me no unity and love for each other from my perspective.

http://www.msn.com/en-gb/news/uknews/tory-eurosceptics-join-calls-for-theresa-may-to-pledge-eu-citizens-can-stay-in-uk-after-brexit/ar-AAnNxbp?li=BBoPRmx&ocid=mailsignout

Tuesday, 7th of March 2017

Well this is interesting, as the news today is that the Brexit bill has been defeated in the House of Lords for a second time. An amendment to the bill has been demanded where there is a clearer picture of Theresa May's final deal with the EU. It looks like more parties and groups want to be informed and involved, and this may be a positive.

The article quotes 'A total of 366 voted for an amendment to the bill to trigger Article 50, with 268 voting against it.'
https://uk.yahoo.com/news/brexit-bill-defeated-second-time-lords-call-meaningful-183700846.html

Wednesday, 8th of March 2017

Today it appears someone has been sacked because of the second defeat that occurred yesterday in the House of Lords over the Brexit. That person is Lord Heseltine and the reason is probably because as a Government adviser he was seen to rebel over the bill. This is what is suggested in the web news article. Please read the article below for more information.

http://www.msn.com/en-gb/news/uknews/lord-heseltine-sacked-by-theresa-may-as-government-adviser-after-rebelling-over-brexit/ar-AAo05eT?li=BBoPWjQ&ocid=iehp

Saturday, 11th of March 2017

While yesterday's news was mainly focused on Lord Heseltine being sacked by Theresa May's government, little is known about Lord Heseltine until yesterday. What is also interesting is that he was hardly even known by the government that employed him. He claims that even though he was a government adviser, he never ever met the Prime Minister, Theresa May. I find that so strange and ironic. I wonder who he was advising then!

https://uk.yahoo.com/news/theresa-may-could-trigger-article-000858759.html

Monday, 13th of March 2017

Today the Brexit Bill faces the final stumbling block as it goes to parliament for what may be the last vote. I think most people, both British and EU citizens just want this over, done and dusted. We need to move to the final stages quickly so everyone knows their fate, both individuals and businesses as well.

http://www.msn.com/en-gb/news/uknews/final-hurdle-for-brexit-bill-as-theresa-may-moves-closer-to-launching-article-50/ar-AAodbCB?li=BBoPRmx&item=personalization_enabled:false

Tuesday, 14th of March 2017

The breaking news today is that the House of Lords have approved the Brexit bill. Theresa May can now trigger Article 50 immediately.

https://uk.yahoo.com/news/may-trigger-article-50-lords-victory-232100438.html

In the meantime the pound has dropped again. This looks like it is going to be a regular event. The news of the Lords brexit vote has had an effect on the pound as it drops to 1.14 against the Euro.

https://uk.yahoo.com/finance/news/pound-plummets-as-lords-vote-in-favour-of-brexit-bill-103052172.html

Last of all Theresa May is planning a tour of the UK to strengthen relationships before she actually triggers Article 50. She will tour Wales, Scotland and Northern Ireland.

https://uk.yahoo.com/news/theresa-may-expected-tour-uk-152638430.html

Thursday, 16th of March 2017

Today there is news that the Brexit Secretary, David Davis has admitted that he is not sure of what will happen if there is no EU deal with the UK. He is simply not sure of the economic impact.

It is clear to me that everything is being done in a rush and a lot of things have not yet been taken into account or thought about properly. This will come to light when Theresa May begins the formal process of withdrawal of the UK from the EU.

https://uk.yahoo.com/news/brexit-david-davis-admits-government-094100873.html

Another article writes that Theresa May has been given the royal backing to trigger Article 50. In other words she has the approval of the Queen. At this point in time we can say that a large majority of the Country are collectively taking responsibility for the Brexit, so at least Theresa can always console herself with the fact that she was only carrying out the will of the people when she triggers Article 50 on the 29th of March 2017 as rumours have it. The 17 million people that voted leave equally need to take responsibility for the Brexit.

http://www.msn.com/en-gb/news/uknews/brexit-bill-granted-royal-assent-giving-pm-power-to-trigger-article-50/ar-BByc1M2?li=BBoPWjQ&ocid=iehp

Monday, 20th of March 2017

Today there is not much in the news regarding Brexit. At the moment we are waiting to hear about the PM's tour round the Country where she will try to build strong support before triggering Article 50 at the end of this month.

One interesting article calls on Theresa May to rethink her Brexit tactic. Apparently she will begin her four-nation tour today and start with Swansea so it will be interesting to see what comes out of that visit. Please see article below for more information.

http://www.msn.com/en-gb/news/uknews/theresa-may-warned-of-looming-battle-over-devolution/ar-BBypaXM?ocid=iehp

Another article talks about the danger of the Brexit affecting science and innovation. At the moment the government has plans for a new industrial strategy and it is trying to spend more on innovation. But a lot of innovation and research funding has actually come from the EU. Will this stream of funding continue after Britain is out of the UK? A lot of scientists and researchers are very worried about the future and the article below has a lot more to say about this issue.

https://www.theguardian.com/business/2017/mar/20/brexit-proof-the-uk-economy-with-more-rd-say-employers

News now confirms that Article 50 will be triggered on the Wednesday the 29th of May 2017. It is said the PM will notify the European Council formally of the objective of the UK leaving the EU. This will begin a 2 year negotiation period of EU withdrawal conversations and by the 29th of March 2019, Britain is expected to finally leave the EU.

This date will be a historic moment in the book of history.

https://uk.yahoo.com/news/article-50-will-be-triggered-on-march-29-downing-street-confirms-113106374.html

Tuesday, 21st of March 2017

I think all the sad Brexit stories are slowly beginning to come to light. A story came to light about Sam Schwarzkopf, a German neuroscientist at University College London. His application for permanent residence was refused even though he has leaved here since 1999 and he is also married to a Britain. He has since then re-applied and it has been approved. However this must have been really stressful. We will probably be hearing more stories of this nature come out after the 29th of March 2017.

https://uk.yahoo.com/news/eu-citizens-uk-anxiously-seek-082102364.html

Another article highlights the concerns of at least 10,000 British pensioners that have relocated to Spain. They are all worried about their future especially with regards to pension and healthcare. It appears many British citizens are worried that they may have no option in the future than to return back to Britain after the Brexit.

That is really an area of concern as they may have invested in property and may lose heavily financially and emotionally if they return back to the UK.

https://uk.yahoo.com/news/british-pensioners-spain-worry-brexit-111712996.html

Wednesday, 22nd of March 2017

So yesterday was one of those days where I tried to follow all the Brexit news but it was over-shadowed with the terrorist attack on Westminster where a total of 5 people died including the attacker and a policeman.

Early on in the morning it was a quiet day filled with the occasional sprinkle of rain. The newspaper had an article of the EU mocking Britain with a cartoon of a boat that was on fire and was sinking in the ocean.

https://uk.yahoo.com/news/eu-mocks-britain-anti-brexit-111122506.html

Another article that was really interesting was titled 'UK-based airlines told to move to Europe after Brexit or lose major routes.'

Major airlines like EasyJet and Ryanair have been advised by the EU chiefs to relocate or risk losing their flying routes in Europe. If you evaluate this you can already see the huge economic impact this will have on Britain. It will affect tourism and masses of jobs as well as ticket price inflation.

https://uk.yahoo.com/finance/news/uk-based-airlines-told-move-093308600.html

Another article that caught my attention was titled 'Tory MPs tell Theresa May to stand firm against EU threat to take Britain to the International Court over £50bn Brexit 'divorce bill'. I personally think politicians and everyone need to wake up to understand that the future problems that we will be facing are more challenging than trying to be rebellious at this point.

The UK need to thread very carefully during their Brexit negotiations and also think very carefully. 17million people have decided to force 43 million people to go down this path and we are now entering into an era of total uncertainty for the future of our future generations in the UK.

http://www.msn.com/en-gb/news/uknews/tory-mps-tell-theresa-may-to-stand-firm-against-eu-threat-to-take-britain-to-the-international-court-over-%C2%A350bn-brexit-%E2%80%98divorce-bill%E2%80%99/ar-BByzr3R?li=BBoPWjQ&ocid=mailsignout

Thursday, 23rd of March 2017

The news about the terrorist attack is plastered on every major reporting newspaper or news website.

There is however a page of public Brexit opinions published in the Metro. Every comment in today's paper responds to the EU responds. Many people agree that people need to wake up and face reality. We cannot have it all. We cannot have an amazing deal if we refuse to agree to the terms of accessing a single market. The PM and her politicians know this but I don't know why people are being given false hope.

There are also reactions about the Brexit result, as some comments say they did not vote but they certainly clearly did not want the Brexit.

http://www.msn.com/en-gb/news/uknews/richard-branson-calls-for-second-eu-referendum-and-says-uk-will-shoot-itself-in-the-foot-with-hard-brexit/ar-BByDBOd?li=AAnZ9Ug&ocid=iehp

Saturday, 25th of March 2017

The final days before Article 50 is triggered is drawing nearer. And just when I thought it would be quiet we already have more Brexit news. The only UKIP MP has resigned today.

https://uk.yahoo.com/news/ukips-only-mp-douglas-carswell-quit-party-120000836.html

Another major headline is about a massive Brexit protest which has happened today. Today is a special day as the EU celebrates its 60th anniversary. There are protests in Rome and other parts of Europe as everyone wants guarantee for their future.

The protesters are marching from Park Lane towards parliament. Many of the protesters are also carrying yellow flowers and the Westminster attack victims and Jo Cox are being remembered.

https://uk.yahoo.com/news/brexit-protests-hundreds-streets-london-121111954.html

Sunday, 26th of March 2017

And there are 2 main Brexit news items today. The first is regarding the European Commission President Jean-Claude Juncker. In an interview, according to him, he is going to ensure that the EU remains stronger when Britain leaves the EU, and other countries will see that leaving the EU is not a good option. So far I think he is suggesting that he is not going to be bending rules during the Brexit negotiation to favour Britain.

https://www.msn.com/en-gb/money/news/eu-chief-juncker-well-make-an-example-of-britain-that-no-one-will-want-to-follow/ar-BByqAH7

EasyJet airlines has also announced it will relocate its European base soon. It states that it should not affect its current head office in Luton where it has about 1000 staff.

https://uk.yahoo.com/finance/news/low-cost-airline-easyjet-close-144900965.html

Monday, 27th of March 2017

Today is the last Monday of EU in freedom in the United Kingdom. Next Monday we will be in a period of post-brexit talks. I therefore rest my pen on the first working day of a week today.

But I cannot rest my pen because the news is flowing. There is some reassuring news as some large firms like Siemens as pledged a long-term commitment to Britain. It is a German engineering group that employs at least 15000 people alone in the UK.

Another German organisation which is the Deutshe Bank has also pledged commitment so it is re-assuring and positive for the employment sector in the UK

Tuesday, 28th of March 2017

Today almost feels like last year. In fact it feels like the 22nd of June 2016 when I was restless and anxious. I remember clearly, how I waited all night and into the morning to wait for the results of the EU referendum

Today however is a different wait. It is the official countdown to the moment Theresa May creates a historic moment by triggering Article 50 which formally begins the 2-year process for Britain to leave the EU.

No one knows what will happen in the months to follow or how this will reshape our lives in the United Kingdom. By the end of the year 2018, the picture may become much clearer.

In the meantime there is an article that talks about how Brexit will affect your holidays in the future in the UK. They forecast that cheap holidays and flights will cease as the speculation is that the pound will continue to slump.

Please read article below;

https://uk.yahoo.com/news/how-will-brexit-affect-my-holiday-to-europe-144419360.html

And the final news for today is Scottish MPs have voted for a second referendum on Scottish independence.

In my opinion, drastic actions create drastic reactions. The main question for many will be that is it possible for Scotland to become independent in the very near future? And if it is, then what about Northern Ireland? We can see that the Brexit decision is slowly reshaping our lives and in years to come we can really look back and understand its full impact.

https://uk.yahoo.com/news/indyref2-vote-msps-back-call-for-second-referendum-on-scottish-independence-161822582.html

Wednesday, 29th of March 2017

And today is a historic moment in Great Britain. The great empire was formed in 1707 and consisted of Scotland, Wales and England. Later in 1801 it merged with Ireland and was then called United Kingdom of Great Britain and Ireland.

In 1973 it became a member of the EEC. And today Theresa May, the United Kingdom's second female Prime Minister, has formally triggered article 50 which begins the formal process for Britain to leave the EU.

She signed a letter which was about 6 pages long, early this morning, which was to invoke Article 50.

The letter was delivered by Ambassador Sir Tim Barrow to the European Council President, Donald Tusk in Brussels around 1.30pm.

If everything goes right and the timetable is on schedule then by March 2019, Britain will cease to become a member of the EU.

https://uk.yahoo.com/news/pm-signs-article-50-letter-call-come-together-004700326.html

http://www.msn.com/en-gb/news/uknews/the-end-of-the-affair-how-the-historic-day-article-50-is-triggered-will-unfold/ar-BByYL8Q?li=BBoPWjQ&ocid=mailsignout

https://uk.yahoo.com/news/article-50-triggered-formal-brexit-process-begins-112600303.html

https://uk.yahoo.com/news/article-50-triggered-formal-brexit-process-begins-112600303.html

Whether this is a terrible or great decision by Britain, this moment will become a historic moment forever in the history of Great Britain.

THE END!

44134220R00078